This Way Once

This Way Once

A Book of Yesterday

An Anthology

Compiled and designed by Annetta Victoria Wood
Illustrated by Ann Oxley

Shepheard-Walwyn
London

First published in 2007 by
Shepheard-Walwyn (Publishers) Ltd
15 Alder Road
London
SW14 8ER
www.shepheard-walwyn.co.uk

British Library Cataloguing in Publication Data
A catalogue record of this book
is available from the British Library

ISBN-13: 978-0-85683-249-9
ISBN-10: 0-85683-249-9

Artistic and Technology consultancy by Bright Future Solutions

Production by Pointing Design Consultancy

Reprographics by GA Graphics

Photograph and copywriting by Paul Heaney

'This Way Once' website by
www.passionfruitdesign.co.uk

Printed and bound in Singapore
by Craft Print International Ltd

Dedication

To My beloved Son, Reginald Heathfield

Whose moments of doubt were only human —
But above all those, kept his faith.

Personal Acknowledgments

With greatest thanks to my son, who gave of His time
and endless knowledge of modern technology, the
means, of bringing my life-time's work to this point.

To Ann, my illustrator, whose ability to interpret my
artistic needs, were profound.

For my family and friends who believed in me,
and to my publisher whose gentle forbearance and
guidance has been much appreciated.

To those great poets, writers and philosophers, whose
works have been a privilege to include, I thank you.

And to my God, who brought me to this place.

And one might therefore say that in this book I have only made up a bunch of other people's flowers, and that of my own I have only provided the string that ties them together.

Michel de Montaigne

11

Contents

I will not bring you flowers,
    but take you by the hand and lead you to
    them –
    Not a fistful of blossom, but a wood dappled
    with primrose shadowed with violets.

    I give you

Pam Brown

... For winter rains and ruins are over
    And all the seasons of snows and sins,
The day dividing lover and lover,
    The light that loses, the night that wins.

And time remembered is grief forgotten
    And frosts are slain and flowers begotten
And in green underwood and cover
    Blossom by blossom the Spring begins.

Algernon Charles Swinburne
'Atalanta in Calydon'

Every valley drinks
Every dell and hollow
Where the kind rain sinks and sinks
Green of spring will follow.

Yet a lapse of weeks —
Buds will burst their edges
Strip their wool-coats, glue-coats,
streaks
In the woods and hedges;

Weave a bower of love
For birds to meet each other
Weave a canopy above
Nest and egg and mother.

Christina Georgina Rossetti
'Winter Rain'

ittle lamb who made thee?
Dost thou know who made thee?

　　Gave thee life and bid thee feed
　　By the stream and o'er the mead;
　　Gave thee clothing of delight;
　　Softest clothing woolly bright,
　　Gave thee such a tender voice
　　Making all the vales rejoice.

Little lamb who made thee?
Dost thou know who made thee?

Little lamb I'll tell thee
Little lamb I'll tell thee

　　He is called by thy name
　　For he calls himself a lamb;
　　He is meek and he is mild
　　He became a little child:
　　I a child and thou a lamb
　　We are called by his name.

Little lamb God bless thee
Little lamb God bless thee.

William Blake

 to be in England
Now that April's there
And whoever wakes in England
Sees some morning unaware.

That the lowest boughs and the brushwood sheaf
Round the elm-tree bole are in tiny leaf
While the chaffinch sings on the orchard bough
In England – now!

And after April, when May follows
And the whitethroat builds, and all the swallows!
Hark, where my blossom'd pear tree in the hedge
Leans to the field and scatters on the clover
Blossoms and dewdrops – at the bent-sprays edge…
That's the wise thrush; he sings each song twice over,
Lest you should think he never could recapture
The first fine careless rapture!
And though the fields look rough with hoary dew
All will be gay when noontide wakes anew
The buttercups, the little children's dower
– Far brighter than this gaudy melonflower!

Robert Browning

O Happy season of the brink
When nature seems to wait and think
        And pays her last adieu:
Then tossing wild across the sky
She seizes spring's embroidery
        And decks herself anew

Peter Leslie

Spring is coming, spring is coming,
    Birdies build your nest;
Weave together straw and feather,
    Doing each your best.

William Blake

For, lo, the winter is past,
The rain is over and gone;
The flowers appear on the earth;
The time of the singing of birds is come.

March brings breezes loud and shrill,
Stirs the dancing daffodil.

April brings the primrose sweet,
Scatters daisies at our feet.

June brings tulips, lilies, roses,
Fills the childrens hands with posies.

Sara Coleridge

I sowed the seeds of love
It was all in Spring
In April, May and June likewise
When small birds they do sing

Anonymous

HOME

This is meeting time again, HOME is the magnet ...
All that is dear, that is lasting, renews its hold on us
We are HOME again ...

Elizabeth Bowen

Home

A world of strife shut out, — a world of love shut in,
The place where the small are great, — and the great are small
The father's kingdom, the mother's world, and the child's paradise —
The place where we grumble the most — and are treated the best
The centre of our affections, around which our heart's wishes twine.

The place where our stomachs get three meals a day
                    And our hearts a thousand
The only place on earth where the faults and failings
Of humanity are hidden under the sweet mantle of charity.

… I have you fast in my fortress
        And will not let you depart,
But put you down into the dungeon
In the round tower of my heart.

And there will I keep you forever,
        Yes, forever and a day,
Till the walls shall crumble to ruin,
And moulder in dust away!

Henry Wadsworth Longfellow
'The Children's Hour'

Sunsets and rainbows, green forest and
Restive blue seas, all
Naturally coloured things are my siblings
We have played together on the floor of the world
Since the first stone looked up
At the stars

Maya Angelou

FOR MY MOTHER

Whose love was the inspiration of this book.

Know I am never far from you,
   I bare you inwardly as you bore me
      – as intimately too,
And as my flesh is of your own
      and our early mesh, woven one, so you are still my own,
And everything about you – home –
      the features – eyes – the hands, your entire form
      are the past, present and to come,
The familiarity, the ease of my living
         And my peace.

Sister Mary Agnes
Order of the Poor Clares

There is a time for some things
And a time for all things
A time for great things
And a time for small things.

To Darling Baby

Where did you come from, baby dear?
Out of everywhere into here —

Where did you get your eyes so blue?
Out of the sky as I came through?

Where did you get that little tear?
I found it waiting when I got here.

What makes your forehead so smooth and high?
A soft hand stroked it as I came by.

What makes your cheek like a warm white rose?
I saw something better than anyone knows.

George MacDonald

31

The Star Fairies

As Ethel lay
    In her cot sleep
She saw the stars
    From their places creep

They frisked and frolicked
    And sang sweet things,
And offered Ethel
    A pair of wings

So she sailed with them
    To the far blue sky
And talked with clouds
    As they floated by;

And filled her hands
    With the moon's soft beams
And travelled long miles
    In the land of dreams

But at break of day
    The stars all fled
And nurse found Ethel
    Asleep in bed.

Noiley Chester

Buttercups

There must be fairy miners
Just underneath the mould,
Such wondrous quaint designers
Who live in caves of gold.

They take the shining metals,
And beat them into shreds;
And mould them into petals
To make the flowers' heads.

Sometimes they melt the flowers,
To tiny seeds like pearls,
And store them up in bowers
For little boys and girls.

And still the tiny fan turns
Above a forge of gold;
To keep with fairy lanterns,
The world from growing old.

Wilfred Thorley

Prayer for a Grandchild

Let no-one hurry her, Lord
Give her the rare, incomparable gift of time
Days to dream, dragonfly days, days when the kingfisher
Suddenly opens for her a window on water
Let no-one chivvy her Lord, let her meander
Lark-happy through childhood, by fern-curled streams
Fringed butter yellow with Kingcups, by secret ways
That paws have worn through the wild
Give her cuckoo loud days and the owl's cry by night.

Dear lord, give her rainbows;
Show her a nest filled with sky-blue promises;
Scoop up for her the sound filled oceans in a shell
Let her keep her dreams,
So that she will always turn her face to the light;
Live merrily, love well;
Hold out ungloved hands to flower and child;
Be easy with animals; come to terms with time.
Lord, let her keep her dreams;
Let her riches be remembered happy days.

Margaret Rhodes

The mother's heart is the child's schoolroom.

Henry Ward Beecher

The beauty of the home is order
The blessing of the home is contentment
The glory of the home is hospitality
The crown of the home is Godliness.

Anonymous

There is always one moment in childhood when
the door opens and lets the future in.

Graham Green

From quiet homes and first beginnings,
 out to the undiscovered ends;
There's nothing worth the winning,
 but laughter and the love of friends.

Friendship

Oh the comfort, the inexpressible comfort, of feeling
safe with a person, having to neither weigh thoughts
nor measure words; but pour them all out, just as
they are, chaff and grain together, knowing that a
faithful hand will take and sift them, keep what is
worth keeping, and then with the breath of kindness,
— blow the rest away.

George Eliot

Kindness is the golden chain
 by which society is bound together.

Johann Wolfgang Goethe

In my father's library words and cadences haunted it
Like song-birds in a magic wood, and I
Wanted to be able to steal away and listen when they called.

Edith Wharton

Flowers seem intended for the solace of ordinary humanity;
children love them, tender contented ordinary people
Love them. They are the cottage's treasure; and in the
Crowded town, mark as with a little broken fragment
Of rainbow, the windows of the workers in whose
Hearts rests the covenant of peace.

John Ruskin

When the voices of children are heard on the green,
And laughing is heard on the hill
My heart is at rest within my breast – and everything else is still

William Blake

The Angel that presided o'er my birth
    Said
Little creature formed of joy and mirth
Go love without the help
    Of anything on earth.

William Blake

I know you wife,
know you as life crumples your clothes,
weaves at your face and passes.
In some part of the milkman's world
you are a smile. Shopkeepers and friends
gleam in its separate lights and think they understand.
All that our children know of you warms them
Like their blankets, tucked by your everlasting hands.
But I, for whom these things mean new expenses
and the loss of you, know you as a bird can know its wings,
a salmon, its return.
You have left sounds in every room protecting me
from loneliness: and if one day I take a car
and find a land to plunder, where your face
does not arrest me like a fundamental law.
Necessity will teach me that your name is love.

Peter Firth

When little things would irk me, and I grow impatient
with my dear ones, make me know how in a moment
joy can take its flight, and happiness be quenched
in endless might. When I would fret and grumble,
fiery hot, of trifles that tomorrow are forgot.
Let me remember Lord, how it would be
If these, my loved ones, were not here with me.

Anonymous

Don't walk in front of me
        I may not follow.
Don't walk behind me
        I may not lead.
Walk beside me
And just be my friend.

To touch the cup with eager lips and taste,
                              not drain it;
To woo and tempt and count a bliss,
                              and not attain it;
To fondle and caress a joy, yet hold it lightly,
Lest it becomes necessity and clings too tightly;
To watch the sunset in the west without regretting,
To hail its advent — in the east, the night forgetting,
To smother care in happiness, and grief in laughter;
To hold the present close, not questioning the hereafter,
To have enough to share, to know the joy of giving,
To thrill with all the sweets of life — that's living.

Robin friend has gone to bed,
Little wings to hide his head.
Mother's bird must slumber, too —
Just as baby robins do.
When the stars begin to rise
Birds and babies close their eyes.

L. Alma Tadema
'Realms of the Unknown Kings'

SUMMER

Summer days for me
When every leaf is on its tree;
When Robin's not a beggar
And Jenny Wren's a bride
When larks hang singing, singing, singing
Over the wheatfields wide —

Christina Georgina Rossetti

Ever drifting, drifting, drifting
     on the shifting
     current of the restless main;
Till in sheltered coves, and reaches
     of sandy beaches,
All have found repose again.

Henry Wadsworth Longfellow
'Seaweed'

She sat, and watched as ...

'Tiny waves ran up onto the shingle, and broke,
And were sucked away again, dragging a rattle of pebbles behind them.'

Rosamunde Pilcher

I meant to do my work today —
But a brown bird sang in the apple tree,
And a butterfly flitted across the field,
And all the leaves were calling me.

And the wind went sighing over the land
Tossing the grasses to and fro
And a rainbow held out its shining hand
So what could I do but laugh and go?

Richard le Gallienne

Happiness is like a butterfly, the more you chase it
the more it will elude you.
But if you turn your attention to other things
It comes and softly, sits on your shoulder.

Here an example from a butterfly
That on a rough, hard rock, happy can lie;
Friendless and all alone
    On this unsweetened stone.

Now let my bed be hard nor care take I,
I'll make my joys like this small butterfly
Whose happy heart has power
    To make a stone a flower.

William H. Davies
'The Example'

To see the world in a grain of sand
And Heaven in a wild flower
Hold infinity in the palm of your hand
And eternity in an hour.

William Blake: 'Auguries of Innocence'

Leisure

What is this life if full of care
We have no time to stand and stare?

No time to stand beneath the boughs
And stare as long as sheep or cows

No time to see when woods we pass
Where squirrels hide their nuts in grass

No time to see in broad daylight
Streams full of stars, like skies at night

No time to turn at beauty's glance
And watch her feet – how they can dance

No time to wait 'till her mouth can
Enrich that smile her eyes began

A poor life this, if full of care
We have no time to stand and stare.

William H. Davies

The little cares that fretted me
I lost them yesterday
Among the fields, above the sea
Among the winds at play
Among the lowing of the herds
The rustling of the trees
Among the singing of the birds.....
The humming of the bees.

The foolish fears of what might pass
I cast them all away
Among the clover-scented grass
Among the new mown hay
Among the hushing of the corn
Where drowsy poppies nod
Where all thoughts die and good are born
Out in the fields with God.

ere in the country's heart
Where the grass in green
Life is the same sweet life
As it e're hath been.

Trust in a God still lives
And the bell at morn
Floats with a thought of God
O'er the rising corn.

God comes down in the rain
And the crop grows tall
This is the country faith
And the best of all.

Norman Gale

I believe a blade of grass is no less than the journey —
work of the stars — And the running blackberry
Would adorn the parlours of heaven.

Walt Whitman

The Way Through The Woods

They shut the way through the woods
    Seventy years ago
Weather and rain have undone it again
    And now you would never know
There was once a road through the woods
    Before they planted the trees
It is underneath the coppice and heath
    And the thin anemonies
Only the keeper sees
    That where the ring-dove breeds
And the badgers roll at ease
    There was once a road through the woods.

Yet if you enter the woods
    Of a summers evening late,
Where the night air cools on the trout-ringed pools
    Where the otter whistles his mate,
(They fear not men in the woods
    Because they see so few),
You will hear the beat of a horses feet,
    And a swish of a skirt in the dew,
Steadily cantering through
    The misty solitudes,
As though they perfectly knew
    The old lost road through the woods...
But there is no road through the woods

Rudyard Kipling

A garden – the place
Where good men disappointed in the quest
Of wealth and power and honours, long for rest
Or having known the splendours of success
Sigh for the obscurities of happiness.

William Wordsworth

Wild Flowers

They were everywhere, scattered freely
blue and white
like bits of broken sky. The heaven's tones
of cloud and air above us matched exactly.
cheerful, common, little weedy faces
up-turned in cool deep grass,
uncultivated,
waiting to be found by whoever came to find them
like all the happiness the world around.

R. H. Grenville

Those happy days that all too quickly pass ...
where treasure lurks 'neath every blade of grass.

When we are green, we ask to be loved.
When we are wise, we ask to be let to love.
To be let to love – it is the reason for living –
The greatest good thing in life.
To love and be loved – that is paradise.

LOVE AND LOSS

Across the gateway of my heart
        I wrote, 'No thoroughfare',
But love came laughing by, and cried
        I enter everywhere.

Herbert Shipman

Friendship is the shadow at evening —
        it grows until the sun of life sets.

Jean de Lafontaine

I think I have felt love most strongly,
not when with a woman, but when I have been
somewhere alone, and free of doubts and
petty problems, have noticed the world growing
brighter. In those moments things have not
changed, but I have been lifted, however briefly
from a world in which everything is temporary
to one that is permanently whole.

Brian Patten

How do I love thee? Let me count the ways
I love thee to the depth and breadth and height
My soul can reach, when feeling out of sight
For the end of being and ideal grace
I love thee to the level of every day's
Most quiet need, by sun and candlelight
I love thee freely, as men strive for right
I love thee purely, as they turn from praise
I love thee with the passion put to use
In my old griefs, and with my childhood's faith
I love thee with a love I seemed to lose
With my lost saints – I love thee with the breath
Smiles, tears of all my life:- and, if God choose,
I shall but love thee better after death.

Elizabeth Barrett Browning

When you are old and grey and full of sleep
And nodding by the fire, take down this book,
And slowly read, and dream of the soft look
Your eyes had once, and of their shadows deep;

How many loved your moments of glad grace,
And loved your beauty with love false or true,
But one man loved the pilgrim soul in you,
And loved the sorrows of your changing face;

And bending down beside the glowing bars
Murmer, a little sadly, how love fled
And paced upon the mountains overhead
And hid his face amid a crowd of stars.

W.B. Yeats

Renouncement

I must not think of thee; and tired yet strong,
I shun the thought that lurks in all delight –
The thought of thee – and in the blue Heaven's height,
And in the sweetest passage of a song

Oh, just beyond the fairest thoughts that throng
This breast, the thought of thee waits hidden yet bright,
But it must never, never come in sight;
I must stop short of thee the whole day long

But when sleep comes to close each difficult day,
When night gives pause to the long watch I keep,
And all my bonds I need must loose apart,
Must doff my will as raiment – laid away –
With the first dream that comes with the first sleep
I run, I run, I am gathered to thy heart.

Alice Meynell

After that moment when at last you let
The whole thing out, the grievances, the fear,
Did you then find it could all disappear,
Clothed in the kindly words, 'forgive, forget'?

It was not so, you only felt the shame
Of being caught out in a hopeless hour
Of being once again within men's power,
A pawn, a puppet in a grown-up game.

Yet if you loved them and they loved you
Beyond the carefully chosen words, the wide
Disarming land where terror seemed to hide
But could not, would the older wish come true?

Elizabeth Jennings

 will not write a poem for you
Because, a poem, even the loveliest
Can only do what words can do –
Stir the air, and dwindle, and be at rest.

Nor will I hold you with my hands, because
The bones of my hands on yours would press
And you'd say after 'Mortal was
And crumbling, that lovers tenderness'.

But I will hold you in thought without moving
Spirit or desire or will –
For I know no other way of loving
That endures when the heart is still.

Humbert Wolfe

It may not always be so, and I say

that if your lips, which I have loved, should touch

  another's, and your dear strong fingers clutch

his heart, as mine in time not far away;

  If on another's face your sweet hair lay

in such silence as I know, or such

  great writhing words as, uttering overmuch

stand helplessly before the spirit at bay;

  If this should be, I say if this should be —

You of my heart, send me a little word;

  that I may go unto him, and take his hands,

saying, Accept all happiness from me.

  Then shall I turn my face and hear one bird

sing terribly afar in the lost lands

  Ah, that you of my heart send me a little word

  is something very precious.

E.E. Cummings

Ah, how skillful grows the hand
That obeyeth love's command;
It is the heart and not the brain
That to the highest doth attain
And he who followeth love's behest
Far exceedeth all the rest,

William Wadsworth Longfellow

The night has a thousand eyes
    And the day but one
Yet the light of the bright world dies
    With the dying sun.

The mind has a thousand eyes
    And the heart but one
Yet the light of a whole life dies
    When a love is done.

Francis William Bourdillon

Farewell to a Little Boy

Honey, there will be a hoop and hills to
      roll it down...
God couldn't give a little boy the burden
      of a crown.
He'll show you lots of trees to climb and
      where he keeps the swings
God, let him have a ball and bat
      instead of shining wings
And will he let you sail a kite up where
      the sky is clear
Without tall buildings stooping down? Of
      course he will, my dear.
Now close your eyes ... I'll kiss them
      shut the way I always do
I must not ... Must not cry, dear God,
      until he's safe with you.

Stop all the clocks, cut off the telephone,
prevent the dog from barking with a juicy bone.
Silence the pianos and with muffled drum
Bring out the coffin, let the mourners come.

Let aeroplanes circle, moaning overhead,
scribbling on the sky the message 'He is Dead',
Put the crepe bows round the white necks of the
    public doves,
Let the traffic policemen wear black cotton gloves.

He was my North, my South, my East and West
My working week and my Sunday rest,
My noon, my midnight, my talk, my song;
I thought that love would last forever – I was wrong.

The stars are not wanted now, put out every one;
Pack up the moon and dismantle the sun,
Pour away the ocean and sweep up the wood;
For nothing now can ever come to any good.

W.H. Auden

FOR ALL OUR LITTLE ONES

Tiny Tim
16.12.1984 – 23.03.1995

Where are you now, my little one, my darling Tiny Tim?
I'm up here Mama, safe and sound, away from all the sin.
I miss you so, my little one, the days seem oh so long!
T'will not be then forever that we unite in song.

You see I'm up in Heaven now, where all is pure and white
Where silver bells bring morning, and golden chimes the night,
I get my titbits just the same, from many Angels' hands;
                              And scoldings too –
But Heaven's a very happy place, content with dreams of you.

I live with your own dear Mother now, where we walk and play each day
So many friends and family, who will never fade away.
All my brothers, sisters, cousins whom I never knew I had
Please believe me earthly mother, it really isn't bad.

I want you to know I'm safe now, that you're not to grieve e're long
That Heaven's a vast vast mansion with gardens broad and strong
Refuge for the weary and solace for all souls
Where you must understand the question that everyone here well knows.

That the span of life on earth is a short one and I was much blessed by you
Not so for all the little ones whose bad luck a short straw drew.
But there's an end to all suffering and beyond where you still are –
There's a world you cannot dream of – yet dear, it is not so far.

So close your eyes this night – my love, with all fears gone away
Be restful through the darkness, until the break of day.
I am your little dog that rests with God, and loves you just the same
Put away those tears and count the years, wherein there rests no blame
I was the happiest of my breed and you were my mistress true
So I play with my toys and I think of my joys, until I'm safe with you.

Annetta Victoria Wood
23rd February 1996

THE QUESTION

I AM ... In every Religion
as a thread through a string
of pearls.

Hindu

71

I said, 'let me walk in the fields',
        God said, 'no, walk in the town',
I said, 'there are no flowers there',
        He said, 'no flowers, but a crown',
I said, 'but the air is thick, there is nothing but drone and din',
        He wept as He sent me back,
        'There's more, He said, there is sin',
I said, 'but the sky is black, and the fogs are veiling the sun',
He answered, 'Yet souls are sick, and souls in the dark undone'.

I pleaded for time to be given,
        He said, 'It is hard to decide, it will not seem
Hard in Heaven, to follow the steps of your guide',
I took one look at the fields, then set my face to the town,
He said, 'My child do you yield, will you leave the flowers
        for the crown'
Then into his Hand went mine ... and into my heart came He,
And I walked in the light Divine
        The path that I feared to see.

Thou shalt know Him when He comes
Not by any din of drums
Nor the vantage of his airs
Nor by anything he wears;
Nor by His crown
Nor his gown
For his presence known shall be
By the Holy harmony
That His coming makes in thee

So many Gods, so many creeds
    So many paths that wind and wind
While just the art of being kind
    Is all the sad world needs.

Ella Wheeler Wilcox

Laugh and the world laughs with you,
    Weep and you weep alone
For the sad old earth must borrow its mirth
    But has trouble enough of its own.

These Two

All people are worth loving.

But the man who goes down to the shore
And tries to weave a rope
From grains of sand, so that – throwing it round
The moon's neck as she surfaces
From the waves – he can rise in the sky;
And the man who bent over a golden river
Spends all his life modelling it – into the form
Of the figureless wind,
To give this world a new courage;
– these two above all others have the right
to live in the tent of my shadow.

When I am absent, know that they are at home.

Stefan Doinas

In a Church

Often I try to analyse
The quality of its silence
Is this where God hides from my searching?
I have stopped to listen, after the few people have gone,
To the air recomposing itself for vigil. It has waited
like this since the stones grouped themselves about it.
These are the hard ribs of a body that our prayers
have failed to animate. Shadows advance from
their corners to take possession of places the
light held for an hour. The bats resume their
business. The uneasiness of the pews ceases.
There is no other sound in the darkness but
the sound of a man breathing, testing his faith on
emptiness, nailing his questions one by one
to an untenanted cross.

R.S. Thomas

Do all the good you can
By all the means you can
In all the ways you can
In all the places you can
At all the times you can
To all the people you can
As long as ever you can.

John Wesley

For now the unborn God in the human heart
knows for a moment all sublimities ...
Old people at evening sitting in the doorways
See in a broken window of the slum
The burning bush reflected, and the crumb
for the starving bird is part of the Broken Body
Of Christ who forgives us — He with the bright hair
— The Sun whose body was spilt on our fields
To bring us harvest.

Edith Sitwell

Dear Father, hear and bless
Thy beasts and singing birds
And guard with tenderness
Small things that have no words.

Anonymous

He prayeth best who loveth best
All things both great and small,
For the dear God who loveth us
He made and loveth all.

Samuel Taylor Coleridge

Those who have heard God speak, can bear His silence.

Listen to the exhortation of the dawn!
Look well to this day! For it is life
  The very life of life.
In its brief course, lie all the verities
  And the realities of your existence.
      The bliss of growth
      The glory of action
      The splendour of beauty
For yesterday is but a dream
  And tomorrow is only a vision;
  But today well lived
Makes every yesterday a dream of happiness
  And every tomorrow a vision of hope
Look well, therefore to this day!
Such is the salutation of the dawn.

Sanskrit

There was a knight of Bethlehem whose wealth
                    Was tears and sorrows;
His men-at-arms were little lambs, his trumpeters
                    were sparrows;
His castle was a wooden cross whereon he hung so high,
His helmet was a crown of thorns whose crest
                    did touch the sky.

He that is thy friend indeed, He will help thee
                    In thy need
If thou sorrow, He will weep, if thou wake,
                    He cannot sleep;
Thus of every grief in heart, He with thee will
                    Bare a part.
These are certain things to show, faithful friend
                    from faltering foe.

Expecting Him, my door was open wide:
Then I looked round
If any lack of service might be found,
And saw Him at my side:
How entered, by what secret stair,
I know not, knowing only He was there.

Thomas Edward Brown

I AM ALPHA AND OMEGA

The beginning and the end
The first and the last.

Revelations

AUTUMN

Even if something is left undone, everyone must take
time to sit still and watch the leaves turn.

Elizabeth Lawrence

Art thou the bird whom man loves best;
The pious bird with the scarlet breast?
Our little English robin;
The bird that comes about our doors
When Autumn winds are sobbing.
The bird who by some name or other
All men who know thee call their brother.

William Wordsworth

Something told the wild geese
　　　it was time to go.
Though the fields lay golden
　　　something whispered 'snow'.
Leaves were green and stirring
　　　Berries, lustre-glossed,
But beneath warm feathers
　　　Something cautioned, 'frost'.
All the sagging orchards
　　　steamed with amber spice
But each wild breast stiffened
　　　At remembered ice
Something told the wild geese
　　　It was time to fly —
Summer sun was on their wings
　　　Winter in their cry.

Rachel Field

The Diary of a Church Mouse

Here among long-discarded cassocks
Damp stools, and half-split open hassocks,
Here where the Vicar never looks
I nibble through old service books.
Lean and alone I spend my days
Behind this Church of England baize,
I share my dark forgotten room
With two oil-lamps and half a broom.
The cleaner never bothers me
So here I eat my frugal tea,
My bread is sawdust mixed with straw,
My jam is polish for the floor.

Christmas and Easter may be feasts
For congregations and for priests,
And so may Whitsun,
All the same they do not fill my meagre frame,
For me the only feast at all
Is Autumn's Harvest Festival,
Where I can satisfy my want
With ears of corn around the font.
I climb the eagle's brazen head
I scramble up the pulpit stair
And gnaw the marrows hanging there.

It is enjoyable to taste,
These items ere they go to waste,
But how annoying when one finds
The other mice with pagan minds
Come into church my food to share
Who have no proper business there,
Two field mice who have no desire
To be baptised, invade the choir ...

...A large and most unfriendly rat
Comes in to see what we are at.
He says he thinks there is no God
And yet he comes ... it's rather odd.
This year he stole a sheaf of wheat
(It screened our special preacher's seat).
And prosperous mice from fields away
Come in to hear the organ play,

And under cover of its notes
Ate through the alter's sheaf of oats.
A low church mouse who thinks that I
Am too papistical, and high,
Yet somehow doesn't think it wrong
To munch through Harvest Evensong.
While I, who starve the whole year through
Must share my food with rodents who
Except at this time of year
Not once inside the church appear.

Within the human world I know
Such goings-on could not be so,
For human beings only do
What their religion tells them to.
They read the bible every day
And always, night and morning, pray
And just like me, the good church mouse
Worship each week in God's own house.

But all the same it's strange to me
How very full the church can be
With people I don't see at all
Except at Harvest Festival.

John Betjeman

But pleasures are like poppies spread –
You seize the flower, its bloom is shed:
Or like the snow falls in the river
A moment white, then melts forever.

Robert Burns
'Tam O'Shanter'

A TRIBUTE

They shall not grown old, as we that are left grow old
Age shall not weary them, nor the years condemn.
At the going down of the sun and in the morning
We will remember them.

Laurence Binyon

Fall, leaves, fall, die, flowers, away:
Lengthen night and shorten day,
Every leaf speaks bliss to me,
Fluttering from the autumn tree.
I shall smile when wreaths of snow
Blossom where the rose should grow,
I shall sing when night's decay
Ushers in a drearier day.

Emily Brontë

... I love the fitful gust that shakes
The casement all the day
And from the mossy elm tree takes
The faded leaf away.
Twirling it by the window pane
With thousand others down the lane.

John Clare
'Autumn'

Bright yellow, red and orange
        The leaves come down in hosts;
The trees are Indian princes,
        But soon they'll turn to ghosts;
The leathery pears and apples
        Hang russet on the bough,
It's Autumn, autumn, autumn late
        Twill soon be winter now.

William Allingham
'Robin Redbreast'

I saw old Autumn in the misty morn
Stand shadowless like silence, listening
to silence ...

Thomas Hood

We never miss the music ... till the sweet-voiced
bird has flown.

REALISATION

Love is not a legend
    Hate is not a certainty
        Otherwise you cannot find the difference
            Between tomorrow and yesterday —

    How can you live then
    If all is dust?

Past and Present

I remember, I remember
The house where I was born,
The little window where the sun
Came peeping in at morn,
He never came a wink too soon
Nor brought too long a day,
But now, I often wish the night
Had borne my breath away.

I remember, I remember
The roses red and white,
The violets and the lily-cups –
Those flowers made of light!
The lilacs where the robins built
And where my brother set
The laburnum on his birthday –
The tree is living yet!

I remember, I remember
Where I was used to swing
And thought the air would rush as fresh
To swallows on the wing,
My spirit flew in feathers then
That is so heavy now
And summer pools could hardly cool
The fever on my brow.

I remember, I remember
The fir trees dark and high
I used to think their slender tops
Were close against the sky.
It was a childish ignorance
But now 'tis little joy
To know I'm farther off from Heaven
Than when I was a boy.

Thomas Hood

... Thanks to the human heart by which we live
Thanks to its tenderness, its joys and fears.
To me the meanest flower that blows can give
thoughts that do often lie too deep for tears.'

William Wordsworth
'Intimations of immortality'

A Robin Redbreast in a cage
Puts all of Heaven in a rage ...

A skylark wounded in the wing –
A Cherubim does cease to sing ...

He who shall hurt the little wren
Shall never be beloved by men.

William Blake

To my Son,

His father's favourite poem, and my son's inheritance.

If

If you can keep your head when all about you
    Are losing theirs and blaming it on you,
If you can trust yourself – when all men doubt you
    But make allowance for their doubting too,
If you can wait and not be tired by waiting
    Or being lied about, don't deal in lies
Or being hated, don't give way to hating
    And yet don't look too good, nor talk too wise;

If you can dream – and not make dreams your master
    If you can think – and not make thoughts your aim,
If you can meet with triumph and disaster
    And treat those two impostors just the same,
If you can bear to hear the truth you've spoken
    Twisted by knaves to make a trap for fools
Or watch the things you gave your life to, broken
    And stoop and build 'em up with worn out tools;

If you can make one heap of all your winnings
    And risk it on one turn of pitch and toss,
And lose and start again at your beginnings
    And never breath a word about your loss:
If you can force your heart and nerve and sinew
    To serve your turn long after they are gone
And so hold on when there is nothing in you
    Except the will which says to them, 'Hold on!'

If you can talk with crowds and keep your virtue
    Or walk with Kings – nor lose the common touch
If neither foes nor loving friends can hurt you
    If all men count with you, but none too much
If you can fill the unforgiving minute
    With sixty seconds' worth of distance run
Yours is the earth and everything that's in it
    And – which is more – you'll be a man, my son!

Rudyard Kipling

Shadow and sun - so too our lives are made –
    Here learn how great the sun, how small the shade.

The music in my heart I bore,
        Long after it was heard no more.

                                William Wordsworth

Hope is the thing with feathers
That perches in the soul,
And sings the tune without the words
And never stops at all.
And sweetest in the gale is heard
And sore must be the storm
That could abash the little bird
That keeps so many warm.
I've heard it in the chillest land
And on the strongest sea,
Yet never in extremity
It asked a crumb of me.

Emily Dickinson

If I can stop one heart from breaking
    I shall not live in vain
If I can ease one life the aching
    Or cool one pain
Or help one fainting robin
    Unto his nest again
I shall not live in vain.

Emily Dickinson

We are the music makers
And we are the dreamer of dreams
Wandering by lone sea breakers
And sitting by desolate streams
World-losers and world-forsakers
On whom the pale moon gleams
Yet we are the movers and shakers
Of the world forever, it seems.

With wonderful deathless ditties
We build up the world's great cities
And out of a fabulous story
We fashion an empire's glory
One man with a dream, at pleasure
Shall go forth and conquer a crown
And three with a new songs measure
Can trample an empire down

We in the ages lying
In the buried past of the earth
Built Nineva with our sighing
And Babel itself with our mirth
And o'er threw them with prophesying
To the old of the new world's worth
For each age is a dream that is dying
Or one that is coming to birth.

Arthur William Edgar O'Shaughnessy

The Old Song

When all the world is young, lad,
And all the trees are green,
And every goose a swan, lad,
And every lass a queen,
Then hey for boot and horse, lad,
And around the world away,
Young blood must have its course, lad,
And every dog his day.

When all the world is old, lad
And all the trees are brown,
And all the sport is stale, lad,
And all the wheels run down,
Creep home and take your place there,
The spent and maimed among,
God grant you find one face there,
You loved when all was young.

Charles Kingsley

Gather ye rosebuds while ye may,
Old time is still a flying,
And this same flower that smiles today,
Tomorrow will be dying

The glorious lamp of heaven, the sun,
— The higher he's a-getting,
The sooner will his race be run
And nearer he's to setting.

The age is best which is the first,
When youth and blood are warmer
But being spent, the worse, and worst
Times still succeed the former.

Then be not coy, but use your time
And while ye may, go marry,
For having lost but once your prime
You may forever tarry.

Robert Herrick

And now here is my secret, a very simple secret,
It is only with the heart that one can see rightly,
What is essential is invisible to the eye.

Antoine de Saint Exupery
'The Fox's advice to the Little Prince'

There is a legend about a bird which sings just once in it's life,
more sweetly than any other creature on the face of the earth.
From the moment it leaves the nest it searches for a thorn tree,
and does not rest until it has found one. Then, singing among
the savage branches, it impales itself upon the longest, sharpest
spine. And dying, it rises above its own agony to
out-carol the lark and the nightingale. One superlative song,
existence the price. But the whole world stills to listen,
and God in His Heaven smiles —

> For the best is only bought at the cost
> of great pain — or so says the legend.

Colleen McCullough
'The Thorn Birds'

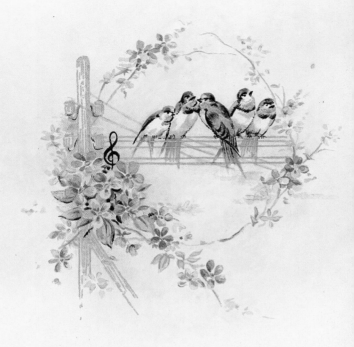

Only one thing matters –
That wherever we go
And however we go
We hear the music of life.

Theodor Fontane

If man does not keep pace
            with his companions, perhaps
It is because he hears a different drummer.
Let him step to the music
            which he hears
However measured or far away …

Henry David Thoreau

If the great beasts are gone
    Man will surely die of a great loneliness of the spirit.

                                        Chief Scattle of the Nez Perce
                                                    1884

Grief

I tell you, hopeless grief is passionless,
That only men incredulous of despair
Half-taught in anguish, through the midnight air
Beat upward to God's throne in loud access
Of shrieking and reproach. Full desertness
In souls, as countries, lieth silent-bare
Under the blanching, vertical eye-glare
Of the absolute Heavens. Deep-hearted man,
    express
Grief for thy dead in silence like to death:—
Most like a monumental statue set
In everlasting watch and moveless woe.
Till itself crumble to the dust beneath.
Touch it: the marble eyelids are not wet:
If it would weep, it could arise and go.

Elizabeth Barrett Browning

The Secret Muse

Between the midnight and the morn,
To share my watches late and lonely,
There dawns a presence such as only
Of perfect silence can be born.
On the blank parchment falls the glow
Of more than daybreak: and one regal
Thought, like the shadow of an eagle,
Grazes the smoothness of its snow.
Though veiled to me that face of faces
And still that form eludes my art,
Yet all the gifts my faith has brought
Along the secret stair of thought
have come to me on those hushed paces
Whose footfall is my beating heart.

Ray Campbell

I have sometimes thought that a woman's nature
is like a great house full of rooms: there is the hall,
through which everyone passes going in and out;
the drawing room, where one receives formal visits;
the sitting room, where members of the family come and go
as they list; but beyond that, far beyond, are other rooms,
the handles of whose doors perhaps are never turned;
no one knows the way to them, no one knows whither they lead;
and in the inner most room, the holy of holies, the soul sits alone
and waits for a footstep that never comes.

Edith Wharton

Remember me when I am gone away,
Gone away into the silent lands,
When you can no more hold me by the hand
Nor I, half turn to go, yet turning stay
Remember me when no more day by day
You tell me of our future that you planned.
Only remember me, you understand
It will be late to counsel then or pray
Yet if you should forget me for a while
And afterwards remember, do not grieve
For if the darkness and corruption leave
A vestage of the thoughts that once I had,
      Better by far that you should forget and smile
      Than that you should remember and be sad.

Christina Georgina Rossetti

Guard within yourself that treasure, kindness,
know how to give without hesitation,
how to lose without regret,
how to acquire without meanness,
know how to replace in your heart,
by the happiness of those you love,
the happiness that may-be wanting for yourself.

George Sand

...What though the radiance that was once so bright
Be now forever taken from my sight;
      Though nothing can bring back the hour
of splendour in the grass, of glory in the flower;
      we will grieve not, rather find
      Strength in what remains behind;
      In the primal sympathy
      which having been must ever be;
      In the soothing thoughts that spring
      Out of human suffering;
      In the faith that looks through death,
In years that bring the philosophic mind.

William Wordsworth
'Intimations of immortality'
from 'Recollections of Early Childhood'.

... We are such stuff as dreams are made on;
and our little life is rounded with a sleep ...

William Shakespeare
Prospero from 'The Tempest'

What should we be without the dolphin's arc
the dove's return ...
these things in which we have seen ourselves
and spoken?

Richard Wilbur

Just living is not enough ...
one must have sunshine, freedom and a little flower.

Hans Christian Anderson

The Fairy Wood

I have grown tired of sorrow and human tears;
Life is a dream in the night; a fear among fears,
A naked runner lost in a storm of spears.

I have grown tired of rapture and loves desire;
Love is a flaming heart, and its flames aspire
Till they cloud the soul in the smoke of a windy fire.

I would wash the dust of the world in a soft green flood;
Here between sea and sea in this fairy wood
I have found a delicate wave-green solitude.

Here, in the fairy wood, between, sea and sea,
I have heard the song of a fairy bird in a tree,
And that peace that is not in the world has flown to me.

Arthur William Symons

Thus times do shift: each thing his turn does hold;
   New things succeed, as former things grow old.

Robert Herrick

The season for kindling the fire
of hospitality in the hall
the genial fire of charity in the heart

Washington Irving

WINTER

On a Cold Day

My sacrament of wine and broken bread
is now prepared, and ready to be done;
The tit shall hold a crust with both his feet
while, crumb by crumb, he picks it like a bone.
The thrush, ashamed of his thin ribs, has blown
his feathers out, to make himself look fat.
The Robin, with his back humped twice as high
for pity's sake – has crossed my threshold mat.
The sparrow's here, the Finch and Jenny Wren,
The wine is poured, the crumbs are white and small –
And when each little mouth has broken bread –
Shall I not drink and bless them one and all.

William H. Davies

Whose woods are these, I think I know
His house is in the village though,
He will not see me stepping here
To watch his woods fill up with snow.

My little horse must think it queer
To stop without a farmhouse near
Between the woods and frozen lake
The darkest evening of the year.

He gives his harness bells a shake
To ask if there is some mistake
The only other sounds, the sweep
Of easy wind and downy flake.

The woods are lovely, dark and deep
But I have promises to keep
And miles to go before I sleep
And miles to go before I sleep

Robert Frost

Now the snow is on the ground
We hardly hear a single sound
The robin is the only bird
That cares to sing a cheery word.

He sits there on the leafless tree
So close at hand that you may see
The movement of his pretty throat
That lifts and falls with every note.

I think I know the reason why
He sings when other birds are shy
It is the fire upon his breast
That keeps him warmer than the rest.

F. Wyville Home

Communique

The stars, with icy unconcern,
Look down upon the earth tonight
And give no sign that prayers are heard
Or hint that things will come out right;
But something in their being there,
Unchanged, through all the change men fear,
In itself the mystic word
That hope has stilled itself to hear.

R.H. Grenville

The Darkling Thrush

I leant upon a coppice gate
  Where frosts were spectre-grey
And winter's dreams made-desolate
  The weakening eye of day
The tangled bine-stems scored the sky
  Like strings of broken lyres
And all mankind that haunted nigh
  Had sought their household fires

   The land's sharp features seemed to be
    The century's corpse outleant
   His crypt the cloudy canopy
    The wind his death lament
   This ancient-pulse of germ and birth
    Was shrunken hard and dry
   And every spirit upon earth
    Seemed fervourless as I.

At once a voice arose among
  The bleak twigs overhead
In a full-hearted evensong
  Of joy unlimited
An aged thrush, frail, gaunt and small
  In blast-be-ruffled-plume
Had chosen thus to fling his soul
  Upon the growing gloom

   So little cause for carolling
    Of such ecstatic sound
   Was written on terrestrial things
    Afar or nigh around
   That I could think there trembled through
    His happy goodnight air
   Some blessed hope, whereof he knew
    And I was unaware.

          Thomas Hardy

Fires Crackle and
Seem to
Burn forever; snow
Falls
Freely, and flakes
Dangle
Deliciously on branches.
Hungry frost
Eats the grass and
Huge rivers freeze; clouds cry quietly
But the tears are trapped
And sunshine
Glistens on the ice while
Ears go red;
Fingers freeze, and
The world turns white.

George Hawkes Dawson
Aged 11

Hark! the Herald Angels

Love came down at Christmas
Stars and Angels gave the sign ....

Christina Georgina Rossetti

CHRISTMAS

The House of Christmas

To an open house in the evening
Home shall men come
To an older place than Eden
And a taller town than Rome
To the end of the way of the wandering star
To the things that cannot be and are
To the place where God was homeless
And all men are at home.

G. K. Chesterton

I saw a stable, low and very bare,
    A little child in a manger,
The oxen knew Him, had Him in their care,
    To men he was a stranger.
The safety of the world was lying there,
    And the world's danger.

Mary Elizabeth Coleridge

... And is it true? And is it true,
  This most tremendous tale of all
Seen in a stained-glass window's hue,
  A baby in an ox's stall?
The maker of the stars and sea
  Become a child on earth for me?

And is it true? For if it is,
  No loving fingers tying strings,
Around these tissued fripperies,
  The sweet and silly Christmas things,
Bath salts and inexpensive scent,
  And hideous tie so kindly meant.

No love that in a family dwells,
  No carolling in frosty air,
Nor all the steeple-shaking bells,
  Can with this single truth compare –
That God was man in Palestine
  And lives today in Bread and Wine.

Sir John Betjeman
From 'Christmas'

For my niece, Hol Pol,

You tear apart the babies rattle, you see what
makes the noise inside.
But there is a veil covering the unseen world, that
not the strongest man could tear apart.

Only Faith, Poetry, Love and Romance can
push aside that curtain and view the beauty in
that glory beyond.

Is it all real?

Virginia, in all this world, in all this world
there is nothing else real in the body. Through Santa
Claus thank God he lives, he lives forever, a thousand
years from now, ten thousand, ten times ten thousand
years from now ….

He will continue to make glad the heart of childhood.

The Editor's reply, from the New York Sun
21 September 1897
To Virginia O'Hanlon, 115 West 95th Street,
New York
'Please tell me the truth, Is there a Santa Claus?'

In the bleak mid winter
    Frosty wind may moan
Earth stood hard as iron
    Water like a stone
Snow had fallen, snow on snow,
    Snow on snow
In the bleak mid winter
    Long ago.

Our God, heaven cannot hold Him
    Nor earth sustain;
Heaven and earth shall flee away
    When he comes to reign;
In the bleak mid winter
    A stable place sufficed
The Lord God Almighty
    Jesus Christ –

    – What can I give Him
        Poor as I am?
    If I were a shepherd
        I would bring a lamb;
    If I were a wise man
        I would do my part –
    Yet what can I give Him
        Give my heart.

Christina Georgina Rossetti
From 'A Carol'

The Oxen

Christmas Eve, and twelve of the clock,
    'Now they are all on their knees',
An elder said as we sat in a flock
    By the embers in hearthside ease.

We pictured the meek mild creatures where
    They dwelt in their strawy pen,
Nor did it occur to one of us there
    To doubt they were kneeling then.

So fair a fancy few would weave
    In these years! Yet I feel,
If someone said on Christmas Eve
    'Come, see the oxen kneel

In the lonely barton by yonder coomb
    Our childhood used to know.'
I should go with him in the gloom
    Hoping it might be so.

Thomas Hardy

The Christmas Tree

 At last there is the tree ...

t last there is the tree ...

Suppose then it has been reserved for this evening,
decorated and kept behind locked doors for this hour
when the children enter the room, it is already
alight, and all other lights are extinguished, found
there like a presence already arrived and
serenely awaiting them, patient in splendour,
becalming at first, or almost hypnotic, it needs only to be
looked at. Even to the older eyes it seems to be
more than it is, more than a conifer covered with objects of
metal and glass and wax, this image of a tree
whose buds are flowers, flowering at mid winter, a tree
burning and unconsumed, evocative of the flowering baytree,
and the burning bush of the mystical
'Dream of the Rood', the tree of Calvary itself, whose
shadow is faint but indelible across the lights
of the Nativity.

Laurence Whistler

How far is it to Bethlehem?
Not very far
Shall we find a stable-room
Lit by a star?

Can we see the little child
Is He within?
If we lift the wooden latch
May we go in?

May we stroke the creatures
there,
Ox, ass or sheep?
May we peep like them and see
Jesus asleep?

If we touch his tiny hand
Will he awake?
Will he know we've come so far?
Just for His sake?

Great Kings have precious gifts
And we have nought
Little smiles and little tears
Are all we brought.

For all weary children
Mary must weep,
Here on His bed of straw
Sleep, children, sleep.

God in His mother's arms,
Babies in the byre,
Sleep, as they sleep who find
Their hearts desire.

Frances Chesterton

HOW FAR IS IT TO BETHLEHEM

May we peep like them and see Jesus asleep?

Everywhere, everywhere, Christmas tonight!
Christmas in the lands of fir tree and pine,
Christmas in the lands of the palm tree and the vine,
Christmas where snow peaks stand solemn and white,
Christmas where cornfields lie sunny and bright!

For the Christ who comes is the Master of all;
No palace too great and cottage too small ...

Phillip Brooks

...We shall be happy: we shall smile and say,
'these years! It only seems like yesterday
I saw you sitting in that very chair.'
'You have not changed the way you do you hair'
'These years were painful, then.' I hardly know
Something lies gently over them, like snow,
A sort of numbing white forgetfulness....'

And so, goodnight, this Christmas
                              And God Bless!

G. S. Fraser
From a letter written during the Second World War

A SUMMING UP

I have lived and I have loved
I have worked and I have slept
I have sung and I have danced
I have smiled and I have wept
I have won and wasted treasure
I have had my fill of pleasure
And all these things were weariness
And some of them were dreariness
And all these things, but two things,
Were emptiness and pain:
And love — it was the best of them
And sleep — worth all the rest of them.

Charles Mackay

Life! I know not what thou art
But know that thou and I must part
And when or how, or where we met
I own to me's a secret yet.

Life! We've been long together
Through pleasant and through stormy weather
Tis hard to part when friends are dear —
Perhaps 'twill cost a sigh, a tear;
    Then steal away, give little warning.
    Choose thine own time:
Say not Good Night — but in some brighter chime
    Bid me good morning.

A. L. Barbauld

Not 'till the loom is silent
And the shuttles cease to fly,
Shall he unveil the canvas
And explain the reason why
The dark threads are as needful
In the weavers skillful hand
As the threads of gold and silver
In the pattern He had planned.

Anonymous

144

All Sung

What shall I sing when all is sung
    And every tale is told,
And in the world is nothing young
    That was not long since old?

      Why should I fret unwilling ears
        With old things sung anew
      While voices from the old dead year
        Still go on singing too?

A dead man singing of his maid
    Makes all my rhymes in vain
Yet his poor lips must fade and fade
    And mine shall sing again.

      Why should I strive thro'weary
      moons
        To make my music true?
      Only the dead men know the tunes
        The live world dances to.

              Richard le Gallienne

For when the one Great Scorer comes
　　　　To write against your name
He marks – not what you won or lost –
　　　　But how you played the game.

Grantland Rice

Does the road wind uphill all the way?
   Yes, to the very end.
Will the day's-journey take the whole long day?
   From morn to night, my friend.

But is there for the night a resting place?
   A roof for when the slow dark hours begin,
May not the darkness hide it from my face?
   You cannot miss the inn.

Shall I meet other wayfarers at night?
   Those who have gone before.
Then must I knock, or call when just in sight?
   They will not keep you waiting at that door.

Shall I find comfort, travel-sore and weak?
   Of labour ye shall find the sum.
Will there be beds for me and all who seek?
   Yea, beds for all who come.

                    Christina Georgina Rossetti

For my Father,
who sought so long ...

The Question

Will you, sometime, who have sought so long and seek still
in the slowly darkening hunting ground, catch sight some
ordinary month or week of that strange quarry you
scarcely thought you sought — Yourself, the gatherer gathered,
The finder found. The buyer, who would buy all, in bounty
bought — And perch in pride on the princely hand, at home,
And there, the long hunt over, rest and roam.

Edwin Muir

Someday, after we have mastered the winds,
The waves, the tide and gravity, we shall
harness for God the energies of love, then
for the second time in the history of the world
man will have discovered fire.

Pierre Teilhard de Chardin

I believe that when death closes our eyes
We shall awaken to a light, of which our
Sunlight is but the shadow.

Arthur Schopenhauer

SOME THOUGHTS ON ANGELS

The Angels keep their ancient places;
    turn but a stone, and start a wing!
'Tis ye,'tis your estranged faces
    That miss the many-splendoured thing

        Francis Thompson 'In No Strange Land'

Their line is gone out through all the earth
And their words to the end of the world

        Psalm 19

All we know of what they do above
Is that they happy are — and that they love

        Edmund Waller

In the sun that is young once only
Time let me play and be

        Dylan Thomas

If I should die and leave you here a while
    Be not like others, sore undone, who keep
Long vigils by the silent dust and weep.
For my sake turn again to life and smile
    Nerving thy heart and trembling hand to do something
    To comfort other hearts than thine;
Complete these dear unfinished tasks of mine
    And I perchance may therein comfort you.

—The happy plains where I cannot come again.

A. E. Housman

Do not stand at my grave and weep
I am not there, I do not sleep.

    I am a thousand winds that blow
    I am the diamond glints on snow
    I am the sunlight on ripened grain
    I am the gentle autumn rain
        When you awaken in the morning's hush
    I am the swift uplifting rush
        Of quiet birds in circled flight
    I am the soft stars that shine at night.

Do not stand at my grave and cry
I am not there – I did not die.

               Anonymous

Lead, kindly light, amid the circling gloom,
                    Lead thou me on;
The night is dark, and I am far from home,
                    Lead thou me on;
Keep thou my feet; I do not ask to see the distant scene,
                    One step enough for me.
I was not ever thus, nor pray'd that thou shoulds't lead me on;
I loved to choose and see my path; but now lead thou me on.
I loved the garish day, and in spite of fears
Pride ruled my will: remember not past years.
So long thy power hath blest me, sure it still will lead me on,
O'er moor and fen, o'er crag and torrent, till the night is gone;
And with the morn those angel faces smile
Which I have loved long since, and lost a while.

                                        Cardinal Newman

Death is not extinguishing the light,
It is putting out the lamp because the dawn has come.

Rabindranath Tagore

Copyright Acknowledgements

Permission from the following to quote from copyright works is gratefully acknowledged:

Anvil Press Poetry for 'These Two' from 'Alibi and Other Poems' by Stefan Doinas,
       translated by Peter Jay and Virgil Nemoianu, 1975
Brian Patten for the passage from his prose poem
Curtis Brown Group Ltd, London on behalf of the estate of Elizabeth Bowen
David Higham Associates for the poem by Elizabeth Jennings from 'Collected Poems',
       published by Carcanet Press
       for the poem by Edith Sitwell from 'Collected Poems',
       published by Duckworth
       for the lines from Dylan Thomas from 'Collected Poems',
       published by Dent
Egmont Publishers for the lines from 'The Fox's Advice' in 'The Little Prince' by
       Antoine de Saint Exupery
The Estate of Margaret Rhodes for her poem
The Estate of Laurence Whistler for his poem
The Estate of Arthur William Symons for his poem
Exley Publications for the poem by Pam Brown
Faber and Faber for Song IX from 'Twelve Songs' in 'Collected Shorter Poems' 1927-1957
       by W H Auden
       for the poem from the 'Collected Works' of Edwin Muir
George Hawkes Dawson for his poem 'Crazy Christmas'
Harper Collins for the poem by Collen McCullough from 'The Thorn Birds'
Hodder and Stoughton for the extract from 'Coming Home' by Rosamunde Pilcher
John Murray for poems 'The Diary of a Church Mouse' and 'Christmas' from 'Collected
       Poems' by John Betjeman
Peters Fraser Dunlop on behalf of the estate of Humbert Wolfe
Random House Group for 'Stopping by Woods on a Snowy Evening' from 'The Poetry of
       Robert Frost', edited by Edward Connery Lathem, published by
       Jonathan Cape
Shepheard-Walwyn (Publishers) Ltd for 'Christmas Letter Home' by G S Fraser from
       'Return to Oasis'
The Society of Authors as the Literary Representative of the Estates of
       Laurence Binyon
       Richard Le Gallienne
A P Watt Ltd on behalf of Grt inne Yeats for 'When you are Old'

We hope that our apologies may be accepted for any copyright material we have failed to
trace, and would welcome any such information for future reprints.

Index